A COMPREHENSIVE GUIDE TO BUILDING AND MANAGING YOUR OWN VPN SERVER

2

Contents

3

4

5

Presentation

In a period overwhelmed by computerized availability, the requirement for secure and confidential correspondence has never been more basic. Virtual Confidential Organizations (VPNs) have arisen as irreplaceable devices for people and associations trying to shield their web-based exercises from inquisitive eyes. While there is a plenty of VPN administrations accessible, building your VPN server gives an unmistakable arrangement of benefits, offering more noteworthy control, customization, and upgraded security. From the fundamental understanding of what a VPN is to the practical application of various software solutions, the goal of this comprehensive guide is to walk you through the complex process of setting up your VPN server.

1.1 What is a VPN?

At its center, a Virtual Confidential Organization is an innovation that empowers clients to lay out a protected and encoded association over the web. The basic role of a VPN is to make a confidential organization from a public web association, permitting clients to communicate information safely and namelessly. VPNs have become pervasive in the advanced computerized scene, utilized for different reasons going from tying down delicate information moves to bypassing geological substance limitations.

A VPN accomplishes its security by making a passage between the client's gadget and a server, encoding the information that navigates this pathway. This encryption guarantees that regardless of whether captured, the information stays indiscernible to unapproved substances. Besides, VPNs can veil the client's IP address, giving namelessness and improving protection by keeping sites and administrations from following their internet based exercises.

1.2 Why Fabricate Your Own VPN Server?

While various business VPN administrations are promptly accessible, picking to fabricate your VPN server offers a bunch of unmistakable benefits. Control and customization top the rundown, empowering clients to fit the VPN to their particular necessities, carry out security conventions of their decision, and have a more straightforward comprehension of the framework's inward operations. Moreover, self-facilitated VPNs give an additional layer of security, as clients have total possession and command over the server, alleviating concerns connected with outsider information taking care of.

Cost-adequacy is another convincing variable. Building your VPN server can be more efficient over the long haul, particularly for people or independent ventures, as it takes out membership charges related with business VPN administrations. Moreover, the Do-It-Yourself approach permits clients to arrange their VPN server to upgrade execution in view of their novel necessities.

1.3 Essentials

Prior to diving into the complexities of building a VPN server, certain requirements should be thought of. An essential comprehension of systems administration ideas, knowledge of the picked working framework, and fundamental order line capability are useful. In addition, users ought to have access to a server, which may be a dedicated physical server, a virtual machine hosted in the cloud, or even a Raspberry Pi for more modest implementations.

Beyond the technical requirements, the VPN's purpose must be clearly understood. Whether it's for tying down far off associations with a business organization, getting to geo-limited content, or guaranteeing security on open Wi-Fi organizations, characterizing the targets will direct the design interaction.

In the ensuing segments of this aide, we will investigate the different parts of setting up a VPN server, from choosing the proper programming and designing the server to carrying out security best practices and investigating normal issues. You will have the knowledge and abilities to set up a robust and secure VPN that is tailored to your specific requirements by the end of this comprehensive walkthrough.

2. Pick Your VPN Programming

Picking the right VPN writing computer programs is an imperative decision during the time spent building your VPN server. Different programming decisions offer evolving components, execution levels, and straightforwardness of game plan. Coming up next are a few popular choices, each with its own unmistakable characteristics:

2.1 OpenVPN

OpenVPN stands out as one of the open-source VPN solutions that is most widely used and trusted. Lofty for its overwhelming security shows, including SSL/TLS for key exchange, OpenVPN offers cross-stage comparability, supporting Windows, macOS, Linux, Android, and iOS. Because of its flexibility, it is a fantastic choice for a great many applications, including individual use and organizations at the venture level.

The arrangement of OpenVPN incorporates delivering key and support records, and its detached arrangement thinks about customization of encryption estimations and check systems. Its versatility makes it reasonable for cutting edge clients, however the broad documentation and simple to-utilize interfaces likewise make it interesting to individuals who are beginning with VPN server arrangement.

2.2 WireGuard

Is a somewhat new VPN administration that has acquired

fame because of its effectiveness, speed, and straightforwardness. WireGuard improves its security by operating within the Linux component with minimal code complexity. Its display benefits are famous, giving speedier affiliation speeds appeared differently in relation to some traditional VPN shows.

WireGuard is easy to set up, including creating a design document for each client and server. Its lightweight nature and focus on straightforwardness make it a charming choice for clients searching for a state of the art VPN game plan with insignificant above.

2.3 SoftEther VPN

SoftEther VPN is a multi-convention, open-source VPN

application that upholds SSL, L2TP/IPsec, and SSTP. One striking component of SoftEther is its ability to enter firewalls, making it a sensible choice for clients defying network restrictions. It supports a variety of operating systems, including FreeBSD, Windows, and Linux.

SoftEther VPN is set up by designing the important settings and introducing the server programming. Because of its versatility, SoftEther can be utilized for a great many undertakings, including bypassing topographical impediments and safeguarding business network interchanges.

2.4 Various Decisions

A couple other VPN programming decisions deal with express necessities. For instance, Algo VPN is known for its ease and effortlessness of course of action, going with it an amazing choice for juveniles. OpenConnect is another decision that prevails with regards to supporting Cisco's AnyConnect show.

Consider factors like the degree of customization required, compatibility with your chosen operating system, and specific features that meet your needs when selecting your VPN software. Assessing client input, directing documentation, and exploring neighborhood can give huge encounters into the characteristics and limitations of each and every item decision.

In the subsequent region of this associate, we will jump into the foundation and game plan processes for OpenVPN, WireGuard, and SoftEther VPN, offering step by step headings to help you in building your VPN server considering your favored item.

3. Select Your Server Working with Provider

Picking the right server working with provider is an essential stage in building your VPN server. The working with provider you select will influence factors like server execution, resolute quality, and flexibility. Coming up next are ordinary working with decisions to consider:

3.1 Cloud Organizations (e.g., AWS, Purplish blue, Google Cloud)

Cloud expert associations offer versatile and versatile responses for working with your VPN server. Among the key part in this industry are Google Cloud Stage (GCP), Microsoft Sky blue, and Amazon

Web Administrations (AWS). These platforms provide a variety of virtual machine (VM) setups, allowing you to select the resources that meet your server's requirements.

Fast organization, simple versatility, and a pay-as-you-go pricing model are among the advantages of cloud hosting. In addition, cloud service providers frequently have server farms in a variety of locations, allowing you to select a server location that maximizes idle time while adhering to legal and administrative considerations.

3.2 Committed Server Providers

Settling on a serious server provider incorporates leasing a genuine server for prohibitive use. Providers like DigitalOcean, Linode, and Vultr offer an extent of server plans, giving you limitless oversight over the hardware and programming game plan.

For customers who want more personalization and want to avoid potential asset sharing issues with virtual machines, dedicated waiters are reasonable. While gave servers could have a higher straightforward cost stood out from cloud organizations, they can offer better execution for unequivocal use cases.

3.3 Raspberry Pi or Other Single Board laptops

For more restricted size executions or individual use, single-board laptops like the Raspberry Pi can go about as reasonable and energy-successful different choices. These devices are good for running lightweight VPN servers and are particularly sensible for circumstances where low power usage is on a very basic level significant.

Keep in mind that single-board personal computers may have fewer capabilities than dedicated servers or cloud services. Regardless, they can be a great choice for learning and giving various things with VPN game plans a shot a more restricted size.

Think about the accompanying while picking a facilitating administration:

Performance: Check the facilitating supplier's organization capacities and equipment particulars to ensure they meet your VPN server needs.

Scalability: Pick a provider that licenses you to successfully scale resources as your necessities create. This is especially fundamental for associations expecting improvement.

Zones for a server farm: Pick a specialist co-op that has server farms in places that are helpful for your ideal interest group or that follow lawful and administrative prerequisites.

Cost: Examine assessing structures, taking into account the fundamental plan costs as well as advancing useful expenses.

In the going with sections, we will guide you through the most widely recognized approach to setting up your server, whether it's on a cloud stage, a dedicated server, or a single board PC, giving little by little rules considering your picked working with environment.

4. Install Your Server

Installing your server is an essential step in building your VPN. Whether you are utilizing a cloud administration, a committed server, or a solitary board PC, the accompanying general advances will direct you through the arrangement cycle:

4.1 Install the Operating System

Installing the operating system (OS) on your server is the first step. The decision of the operating system relies upon your inclinations and the similarity with the VPN programming you've chosen. Ubuntu, CentOS, Debian, and other options are common. Cloud suppliers frequently give pre-arranged pictures to speedy organization.

Follow these general advances:

Connect the USB or DVD media used for installation to your server.
Boot the server from the establishment media.
Adhere to the on-screen directions to introduce the working framework.

4.2 Arrange Organization Settings

When the operating system is introduced, design the organization settings to guarantee your server has a static IP address. This is essential for keeping a reliable association with your VPN server.

4.3 Update and Redesign Framework Bundles

In the wake of arranging the organization settings, update the framework bundles to guarantee that your server has the most recent security fixes and updates. Depending on your OS, use the following commands:

For Debian/Ubuntu:

slam
Duplicate code
sudo adept update
sudo adept redesign
For CentOS:

This ensures that your server is running the most recent software versions, reducing vulnerabilities.

```bash
Copy code
sudo yum update
sudo yum upgrade
```

In the resulting areas, we will dive into the establishment and setup processes for explicit VPN programming choices, giving bit by bit directions in light of your picked VPN arrangement. Whether it's OpenVPN, WireGuard, or SoftEther VPN, these definite aides will assist you with exploring through the complexities of setting up your VPN server.

Client
Introduce and Design VPN Programming

5. Introduce and Design VPN Programming

The establishment and setup of VPN programming will rely upon the particular arrangement you've decided for your VPN server. The following are bit by bit directs for three well known VPN programming choices: OpenVPN, WireGuard, and SoftEther VPN.

5.1 OpenVPN Establishment and Arrangement

Stage 1: Introduce OpenVPN

For Debian/Ubuntu:

slam
Duplicate code
sudo adept introduce openvpn
For CentOS:

slam
Duplicate code
sudo yum introduce openvpn
Stage 2: Design OpenVPN

Make another catalog to store OpenVPN arrangement records:

slam
Duplicate code
sudo mkdir/and so on/openvpn/server
Duplicate the example design documents to the new index:

slam
Duplicate code
sudo cp -r/usr/share/doc/openvpn/models /simple rsa/2.0/*/and so on/openvpn/server/
Alter the arrangement record:

slam

Duplicate code

sudo nano/and so forth/openvpn/server/server.conf Change setups depending on the situation, including server IP, port, and convention.

Step 3: Produce Testaments and Keys

Explore to the EasyRSA registry:

cd /etc/openvpn/server/easy-rsa/2.0 to copy the code Edit the vars file:

Save the file by using bash, sudo nano vars, and copying the code.

Source the vars document and fabricate the Endorsement Authority:

slam
Duplicate code
source vars
sudo ./clean-all
sudo ./construct ca
Construct the server key:

slam
Duplicate code
sudo ./construct key server
Create Diffie-Hellman boundaries:

slam
Duplicate code
sudo ./construct dh
Stage 4: Begin OpenVPN

Empower IP sending:

slam
Duplicate code
sudo sysctl - w net.ipv4.ip_forward=1
Begin the OpenVPN administration:

5.2 WireGuard Installation and Configuration

Step 1: Copy the code with sudo service openvpn start Introduce WireGuard

For Debian/Ubuntu:

slam
Duplicate code
sudo able introduce wireguard
For CentOS:

slam
Duplicate code
sudo yum introduce wireguard-devices

Stage 2: Design WireGuard

Produce server and client key matches:

slam

Duplicate code
umask 077
wg genkey | sudo tee/and so
on/wireguard/privatekey | wg
pubkey | sudo tee/and so
on/wireguard/publickey
Make the WireGuard arrangement document:

slam
Duplicate code
sudo nano/and so
forth/wireguard/wg0.conf
Add setups, including private key, IP address, and port.

Step 3: Begin WireGuard

Begin the WireGuard interface:

slam
Duplicate code
sudo wg-speedy up wg0

Empower WireGuard to begin at boot:

5.3 SoftEther VPN Installation and Configuration

Step 1: Copy the code using sudo systemctl. Introduce SoftEther VPN Server

Download and remove the SoftEther VPN Server bundle from the authority site.

Run the installer script:

slam
Duplicate code
sudo ./vpnserver start

Stage 2: Access the SoftEther VPN Server Manager for configuration:

slam
Duplicate code
sudo ./vpncmd

Utilize the accompanying orders to design the server:

slam
Duplicate code
ServerPasswordSet
HubCreate YourHubName
UserCreate
YourUserName/Gathering:
none/REALNAME: none/NOTE:
none
UserPasswordSet YourUserName
Stage 3: Begin SoftEther VPN Server

Begin the SoftEther VPN server:

slam
Duplicate code
sudo ./vpnserver start
These guidelines give an essential arrangement to each VPN programming choice. You may need

to modify DNS, firewall rules, and routing settings based on your specific needs and network configurations. Counsel the authority documentation for every product for cutting edge designs and investigating tips.

In the accompanying areas of this aide, we will investigate extra advances, for example, creating authentications, designing firewall settings, and empowering and testing your VPN server.

6. Create Declarations and Keys

Declarations and keys assume a vital part in getting the correspondence between your VPN server and clients. The method involved with producing declarations and keys fluctuates relying upon the VPN programming you're utilizing. The following are ventures for producing testaments and keys for OpenVPN, WireGuard, and SoftEther VPN.

6.1 OpenVPN Authentication and Key Age

Expecting you have previously set up OpenVPN and explored to the EasyRSA index:

Step 1: Produce Endorsement Authority (CA)

slam
Duplicate code
source vars
./clean-all
./assemble ca
Follow the prompts to set up your Authentication Authority.

Step 2: Produce Server Key and Authentication

slam
Duplicate code
./assemble key server
Once more, follow the prompts. The server key and certificate are produced by this.

Step 3: Create Diffie-Hellman Parameters with bash Copy code./build-dh In this step,

additional security is provided by creating Diffie-Hellman parameters.

6.2 WireGuard Key Pair Age

For WireGuard, you'll create public and confidential key matches for the server and every client.

Step 1: Copy code: umask 077 wg genkey | sudo tee /etc/wireguard/privatekey | wg pubkey | sudo tee /etc/wireguard/publickey
Generate Server Key Pair This command generates the server's private and public keys.

Step 2: Produce Client Key Pair (Rehash for Every Client)

slam
Duplicate code

umask 077
wg genkey | tee privatekey | wg pubkey | tee publickey
Rehash this step for every client, producing a remarkable sets of private and public keys.

6.3 SoftEther VPN Authentication and Key Age

For SoftEther VPN, you'll utilize the VPN Server Chief order line instrument to set up endorsements.

Step 2: Access VPN Server Manager via bash Copy the code to./vpncmd Set Up Testament for Server

slam
Duplicate code
ServerCertSet
YourHubName/LOADCERT:
your_server_cert.pem/LOADKEY:
your_server_key.pem
Supplant "YourHubName," "your_server_cert.pem," and "your_server_key.pem" with your ideal qualities.

Step 3: Set Up Declaration for Client (Discretionary)

slam
Duplicate code
UserCertReg
YourUserName/LOADCERT:
/LOADKEY: your_user_cert.pem
your_user_key.pem
This step is discretionary and can be utilized if you have any desire to set up authentications for individual clients.

Guarantee to safely store these created testaments and keys, particularly the confidential keys, as they are critical for the security of your VPN. In the accompanying areas, we will cover designing firewall settings, empowering your VPN server, and making VPN client profiles for secure associations.

7. Configure Firewall Settings

To secure your VPN server, configure your firewall to allow the VPN protocol's required traffic. The particular advances rely upon the VPN programming you're utilizing and the firewall the board instrument on your server. The following are basic rules for designing firewall settings for OpenVPN, WireGuard, and SoftEther VPN.

7.1 OpenVPN Firewall Design

For OpenVPN, you really want to permit traffic on the port determined in your OpenVPN server arrangement (default is UDP 1194). Change the port in the event that you designed an alternate one.

Step 1: Open the Vital Port

slam
Duplicate code
sudo ufw permit 1194/udp
Supplant "1194" with your designed OpenVPN port.

Step 2: Permit Sending

Alter the sysctl.conf document:

slam
Duplicate code
sudo nano/and so on/sysctl.conf
Uncomment the line:

plaintext
Duplicate code
#net.ipv4.ip_forward=1
Reload sysctl:

Copy code with bash sudo sysctl -p

7.2 WireGuard Firewall Configuration To use WireGuard

, you must permit traffic on the port that is specified in your configuration (the default is UDP 51820). Change the port in the event that you designed an alternate one.

Step 1: Open the Essential Port

slam
Duplicate code
sudo ufw permit 51820/udp
Supplant "51820" with your arranged WireGuard port.

7.2 SoftEther VPN Firewall Design

SoftEther VPN commonly involves a few ports for various conventions. Change your firewall settings in view of your SoftEther VPN arrangement.

Step 1: Open Necessary Ports sudo ufw allow 500/udp sudo ufw allow 4500/udp sudo ufw allow 1701/udp sudo ufw allow 443/tcp These commands permit traffic on the SoftEther VPN's common ports.

Step 2: Permit Sending

Alter the sysctl.conf document:

slam
Duplicate code
sudo nano/and so forth/sysctl.conf
Uncomment the line:

plaintext
Duplicate code
#net.ipv4.ip_forward=1
Reload sysctl:

slam
Duplicate code
sudo sysctl - p
In the wake of arranging firewall settings, you can continue to empower and begin your VPN server. Remember that these means could require changes in light of your particular server arrangement and necessities. Continuously allude to the documentation of your picked VPN programming and firewall the board device for exact guidelines. We'll talk about starting and enabling your VPN server, creating VPN client profiles, and putting security best practices into practice in the following sections.

8. Empower and Begin Your VPN Server

Empowering and beginning your VPN server includes guaranteeing that the essential administrations are running and that your server is prepared to acknowledge client associations. The particular steps depend on the VPN software you choose.

8.1 Turn on OpenVPN and Launch It OpenVPN:

Step 1: Empower the OpenVPN Administration

slam
Duplicate code
sudo systemctl empower openvpn@server

This order empowers the OpenVPN administration to begin at boot.

Step 2: Begin the OpenVPN Administration

slam
Duplicate code
sudo systemctl start openvpn@server
This order begins the OpenVPN administration right away.

8.2 Empower and Begin WireGuard

For WireGuard:

Step 1: Empower the WireGuard Administration

slam
Duplicate code

sudo systemctl empower wg-quick@wg0

This order empowers the WireGuard administration to begin at boot.

Step 2: Begin the WireGuard Administration

slam
Duplicate code
sudo systemctl start wg-quick@wg0

This order begins the WireGuard administration right away.

8.3 Empower and Begin SoftEther VPN

For SoftEther VPN:

Step 1: Begin the SoftEther VPN Server

slam
Duplicate code
sudo ./vpnserver start
This order begins the SoftEther VPN server.

8.4 Test the VPN Server Locally

Interface with your VPN server locally utilizing a client on a similar organization. This guarantees that the server is working accurately and that your firewall settings grant neighborhood associations.

8.5 Test the VPN Server From a distance

To test your VPN server from a distance, utilize a client gadget outside the nearby organization.

Associate with the server utilizing the fitting VPN client programming and arrangements. Guarantee that you can lay out a safe association and that information transmission is encoded.

Assuming you experience issues during testing, allude to the logs of your picked VPN programming for blunder messages and investigating data. Misconfigurations of the firewall, mismatches between the certificate and key, and incorrect server configurations are all common problems.

When you've effectively tried the VPN server, continue to the following segments to make VPN client profiles, execute security best practices, and investigate any potential issues that might emerge.

9. Make VPN Client Profiles

Making VPN client profiles includes producing arrangement records or settings that clients will use to associate with your VPN server. The cycle varies for each VPN programming. The following are ventures for making client profiles for OpenVPN, WireGuard, and SoftEther VPN.

9.1 OpenVPN Client Profile Creation

Stage 1: Create Client Endorsement and Key

Accepting at least for a moment that you're still in the EasyRSA registry:

slam

Duplicate code
source vars
./assemble key YourClientName
Follow the prompts to make an endorsement and key pair for your client.

Step 2: Make Client Setup Record

Make another record (e.g., client.ovpn) and add the accompanying substance:

plaintext
Duplicate code
client
dev tun
proto udp
distant YourServerIP 1194
resolv-retry boundless
nobind
continue key
continue tun

comp-lzo
action word 3
ca ca.crt
cert YourClientName.crt
key YourClientName.key
Supplant "YourServerIP" with your server's IP address and change the document names appropriately.

9.2 Creating a WireGuard

Client Profile Each client requires its own distinct configuration file for WireGuard. In the event that you have created the client's key pair:

Step 1: Make Client Design Record

Make another record (e.g., client.conf) and add the accompanying substance:

plaintext

Duplicate code
[Interface]
PrivateKey = YourClientPrivateKey
Address = YourClientIPAddress/32
DNS = YourDNSServer

[Peer]
PublicKey = YourServerPublicKey
Endpoint = YourServerIP:51820
AllowedIPs = 0.0.0.0/0
Supplant "YourClientPrivateKey," "YourClientIPAddress," "YourDNSServer," "YourServerPublicKey," and "YourServerIP" with the fitting qualities.

9.3 SoftEther VPN Client Profile Creation

For SoftEther VPN, you'll utilize the VPN Client Chief or arrange clients physically.

Step 1: Use the VPN Client Manager (Recommended) On the client device, download and install the SoftEther VPN Client Manager.

Select "New Setting" from the File menu when you open the Manager.

Enter a name for the new setting, add your server subtleties, and snap "Make."

Interface with the server utilizing the made setting.

Step 2: Manual Arrangement

Make another association in the SoftEther VPN Client Supervisor:

Send off the chief and snap "New Association Setting."

Enter a name for the setting.

Add your server subtleties in the "Host Name" field.

Pick the fitting VPN convention.

Arrange verification settings (username/secret phrase or endorsement).
Save the settings and associate with the server.
Whenever you've made client profiles, disperse the pertinent setup documents or settings to your VPN clients. Ensure that clients utilize the appropriate connection information, keys, and certificates. In the following segments, we will investigate security best works on, investigating, and extra contemplations for your VPN server.

10. Security Best Practices

Guaranteeing the security of your VPN server is vital to safeguard the secrecy and uprightness of the information communicated through the organization. Here are some security best practices to consider:

10.1 Regular Updates

Ensure that your server's VPN software, operating system, and any other packages that are installed are up to date. Consistently check for security refreshes and apply them quickly to address weaknesses.

On Debian/Ubuntu, for instance, use:

slam

Duplicate code
sudo adept update
sudo adept overhaul
On CentOS, use:

Use Strong Authentication Methods
Use strong authentication methods for both server and client connections. bash Copy code sudo yum update sudo yum upgrade

10.2 Use passwords and username

That are difficult to remember, or think about using certificate-based authentication for extra safety. Also, consider carrying out multifaceted confirmation (MFA) for an additional layer of safety.

10.3 Logging and Observing

Empower logging and routinely audit logs for any uncommon

exercises or potential security episodes. Observing instruments can assist you with following server execution and distinguish dubious examples. Set up alarms for basic occasions to immediately get notices.

10.4 Organization Division

Consider putting your VPN server in a committed organization portion to segregate it from different administrations. This forestalls unapproved admittance to different pieces of your organization in the event of a security break.

10.5 Handicap Pointless Administrations

Handicap any pointless administrations or ports on your

server to decrease the assault surface. Just empower the administrations expected for the working of your VPN server.

10.6 Implement Rate

Limitation Protect authentication mechanisms from brute-force attacks by implementing rate limiting. This keeps an assailant from more than once endeavoring to get entrance by attempting different usernames and passwords.

10.7 Ordinary Reinforcements

Consistently reinforcement your server arrangements, declarations, and keys. In case of a server disappointment or security episode, having forward-thinking reinforcements guarantees a quicker recuperation process.

10.8 Occasional Security Reviews

Direct intermittent security reviews to survey the general security stance of your VPN server. This incorporates evaluating designs, checking for obsolete programming, and guaranteeing consistence with security best practices.

10.9 Encryption and Code Contemplations

Pick solid encryption calculations and codes for your VPN associations. Consistently audit and update these settings in view of the most recent security proposals. Furthermore, debilitate censured or shaky conventions.

10.10 Compliance and Legal Considerations

Be aware of your jurisdiction's data privacy and security laws and regulations. Guarantee that your VPN server arrangement agrees with these guidelines, and go to important lengths to safeguard client information.

Carrying out these security best practices will add to the strength of your VPN server and assist with protecting the information sent through the organization. Routinely audit security rules and remain informed about arising dangers to adjust your safety efforts appropriately.

11. Exploring

Exploring is a central piece of keeping a valuable VPN server. Normal investigating systems for settling issues that might happen during the design or activity of your VPN server are as per the following:

11.1 Truly investigate Logs

Take a gander at the logs of your VPN programming for bungle messages or reprobations. These logs can give critical encounters into the justification for issues. Normal areas for logs include:

OpenVPN:
/var/log/openvpn/openvpn.log
WireGuard: Check the structure logs or use the journalctl request.

VPN SoftEther: Use the vpncmd gadget to see logs.

11.2 Check Firewall Settings

Make sure your firewall's settings are correct. Avow that the significant ports are open, and traffic is considered your VPN show. Use the fitting requests for your firewall the board gadget, whether it's UFW, iptables, or another.

11.3 Client-Side Issues

Expecting clients can't interact, research client-side issues:

Attest that the client plans match the server settings.

Check for any blunders or mistakes in the client configuration records.

Affirm that the client's firewall licenses traffic on the VPN port.

11.4 Issues with Availability

Assuming clients interface yet have network issues:

Check expecting the server's association affiliation is consistent. Avow that the server's public IP is reachable from the web. Ensure that controlling and DNS settings are precisely organized.

11.5 Testament and Key Befuddles

Confirm that the server and client verification authentications and keys match. Ensure that the Ordinary Name (CN) in statements matches the server and client names.

11.6 Assent Issues

Ensure that the assents on fundamental archives and files,

similar to verifications and private keys, are set precisely. For example, classified key records should have restrictive assents (e.g., 600).

11.7 Server Resource Objectives

All things considered take a gander at server resource use, including PC processor, memory, and association information move limit. Resource prerequisites can incite adulterated execution or organization issues.

11.8 Update Programming

Ensure that your server's functioning system and VPN writing computer programs are revived to the latest structures. Bug fixes and security fixes that can take care of issues are every now and again remembered for programming refreshes.

11.9 Review Configuration Records

Circumspectly review your server and client configuration records for goofs or anomalies. Errors or misconfigurations can incite alarming approach to acting.

11.10 Network Packet Analysis

Perform network packet analysis by analyzing network traffic with applications like Wireshark. This can provide insights into correspondence issues and help identify issues at the bundle level.

11.11   Neighborhood   and Documentation

Counsel social class get-togethers, discussion social affairs, or official documentation for the specific VPN writing computer programs you're using. As often as possible, others have encountered similar issues and may give plans or workarounds.

If researching doesn't decide the issue, consider reaching on the web organizations or conversations for help. Make sure to give clear information about the issue, including significant log entries and configuration reports, to work with a more definite end.

12 Considerations

Despite the middle game plan, security endeavors, and researching, the following are a couple of additional considerations to work on the value and comfort of your VPN server:

12.1 Data transmission and Execution

Think about the VPN server's transfer speed necessities and expected use. Bandwidth heightened works out, for instance, streaming or gigantic archive moves, may impact execution. Pick a server with adequate resources, and screen execution estimations reliably.

12.2 Client The Board

Implement a client the board framework if your VPN server will have multiple clients. This can consolidate setting up individual client accounts, giving out unambiguous assents, and keeping a log of client practices for assessing.

12.3 Endorsement Disavowal

If a client's confidential key is compromised, carry out a system for denial of the testament. This guarantees that the testament can be refuted in case of a client's certifications being compromised, forestalling unapproved access.

12.4 Overt repetitiveness and Failover

Think about carrying out overt repetitiveness and failover systems to ensure your VPN administration's consistent accessibility. This could incorporate setting up different servers or utilizing load changing systems to convey traffic.

12.5 VPN Client Plan Items

For client convenience, give clients plan scripts or records that modernize the course of action association. This deals with the affiliation association for end-clients and decreases the likelihood of configuration botches.

12.6 Consistence with Protection

Guidelines On the off chance that your VPN server handles touchy information, ensure it follows any appropriate security regulations, like GDPR, HIPAA, or others.

Execute encryption, data support draws near, and various measures to defend client insurance.

12.7 Geo-Overt repetitiveness

If your VPN serves customers all over the world, you might want to consider distributing servers in a variety of geographical locations. This reduces dormancy and ensures a prevalent client experience for clients communicating from different regions.

12.8 Typical Audits and Overviews

Lead discontinuous surveys and reviews of your VPN server course of action. Client access surveys, execution assessments, and security reviews are instances of this. Standard appraisals help with perceiving potential issues proactively.

12.9 Legitimate and Moral Thoughts

Understand the legitimate and moral thoughts enveloping VPN use in your space. Terms of service or local laws may be violated in certain activities, such as circumventing copyright restrictions or participating in criminal activities.

12.10 Documentation

Stay aware of broad documentation for your VPN server plan. This integrates arrangement records, security draws near, client guides, and any custom contents or gadgets you've completed. For future maintenance and investigation, documentation is crucial.

By considering these additional points of view, you can make an all the more impressive, straightforward, and steady VPN server that meets the specific necessities of your clients and affiliation. Regularly review and update your course of action considering creating necessities and emerging headways.

13. End

Building your VPN server can be a compensating try, giving you more prominent command over your organization security and empowering secure remote access for clients. All through this aide, we've covered key stages, including choosing VPN programming, picking a facilitating supplier, server arrangement, client profile creation, security best works on, investigating, and extra contemplations.

You can create a VPN server that meets your specific needs by carefully following each step and considering security best practices. Ordinary support, updates, and checking will add to the continuous achievement and security of your VPN framework.

As you keep on dealing with your VPN server, remain informed about the most recent advancements in VPN advances, security dangers, and best practices. Draw in with local area gatherings, read documentation, and take part in conversations to profit from the aggregate information on the more extensive local area.

Recollect that security is a continuous cycle, and adjusting to new difficulties is a vital part of keeping a protected and dependable VPN server. Whether you use OpenVPN, WireGuard, SoftEther VPN, or another solution, staying proactive and informed will ensure that your VPN server continues to provide you and your users with a safe and effective means of communication.